G000079030

Liberty Phi

VIRGO

INTRODUCTION

Astrology is all about the planets in our skies and what energy and characteristics influence us. From ancient times, people have wanted to understand the rhythms of life and looked to the skies and their celestial bodies for inspiration, and the ancient constellations are there in the 12 zodiac signs we recognise from astrology. The Ancient Greeks devised narratives related to myths and legends about their celestial ancestors, to which they referred to make decisions and choices. Roman mythology did the same and over the years these ancient wisdoms became refined into today's modern astrology.

The configuration of the planets in the sky at the time and place of our birth is unique to each and every one of us, and what this means and how it plays out throughout our lives is both fascinating and informative. Just knowing which planet rules your sun sign is the beginning of an exploratory journey that can provide you with a useful tool for life.

Understanding the meaning, energetic nature and power of each planet, where this sits in your birth chart and what this might mean is all important information and linked to your date, place and time of birth, relevant *only* to you. Completely individual, the way in which you can work with the power of the planets comes from understanding their qualities and how this might influence the position in which they sit in your chart.

What knowledge of astrology can give you is the tools for working out how a planetary pattern might influence you, because of its relationship to your particular planetary configuration and circumstances. Each sun sign has a set of characteristics linked to its ruling planet – for example, Virgo is ruled by Mercury – and, in turn, to each of the 12 Houses (see page 81) that form the structure of every individual's birth chart (see page 78). Once you know the meanings of these and how these relate to different areas of your life, you can begin to work out what might be relevant to you when, for example, you read in a magazine horoscope that there's a Full Moon in Capricorn or that Jupiter is transiting Mars.

Each of the 12 astrological or zodiac sun signs is ruled by a planet (see page 52) and looking at a planet's characteristics will give you an indication of the influences brought to bear on each sign. It's useful to have a general understanding of these influences, because your birth chart includes many of them, in different house or planetary configurations, which gives you information about how uniquely *you* you are. Also included in this book are the minor planets (see page 102), also relevant to the information your chart provides.

VIRGO

Our sun sign is determined by the date of our birth wherever we are born, and if you are a Virgo you were born between August 23rd and September 22nd. Bear in mind, however, that if you were born on one or other of those actual dates it's worth checking your *time* of birth, if you know it, against the year you were born and where. That's because no one is born 'on the cusp' (see page 78) and because there will be a moment on those days when Leo shifts to Virgo, and Virgo shifts to Libra. It's well worth a check, especially if you've never felt quite convinced that the characteristics of your designated sun sign match your own.

The constellation of Virgo is the second largest in our skies. The fourteen stars form the figure of a human and its brightest star is Alpha Virginis. Virgo represents the Greek winged goddess Dike, who sought to warn the world that after Zeus took power from his father Chronos, life would become violent and warlike, but no one listened. Virgo is Latin for unsullied maiden, symbolising innocence.

Virgo is ruled by Mercury, the messenger of the Gods associated not only with methods of communication but also intelligence and reason, and in this sign brings clarity of mind, decisiveness and diligence.

An earth sign (like Taurus and Capricorn) Virgo can be extremely methodical and pragmatic. They are often more than happy to get their hands metaphorically dirty to get things done, and they love to tick off tasks as they are done. And because they are a mutable sign (like Gemini, Pisces and Sagittarius), they are also adaptable in their attitude, and their practical nature can be quite versatile, which makes many Virgos excellent problem-solvers. This brings more creativity to their approach than most Virgos are usually credited for, because although depicted as a chaste maiden or virgin, Virgo is also about fecundity and gestation, the ability to produce material from ideas. This is hugely beneficial when it comes to getting things done, rather than just talking about them.

The sign ♍ of Virgo shows the reproductive organs but these are represented as closed and untouched. And although she is sexually pure, the virgin is often depicted holding a sheaf of wheat, representing the harvest of ideas that might nourish us.

PHYSICAL POWER
Virgo rules not only the intestines but also the nervous system, which we now know are closely connected, and their gut often responds to their emotions.

SACRED GEMSTONE
The beautiful blue Sapphire which evokes peace and was once thought to be symbolic of hope. It resonates with Virgo's need for self-expression and is also associated with the sort of wealth and abundance that comes from hard work.

OPPOSITE SIGN
Pisces

Virgo is depicted by the chaste maiden, who is sometimes considered to be a little uptight in her attitude, wanting to do things properly and by the book. An earth sign, Virgo is grounded in reality but as a mutable sign, they are in fact much more adaptable to people, places and circumstances than they're usually given credit for.

Virgo is also depicted as holding a sheaf of wheat or cereal, showing the abundance that can come from sowing a seed in fertile ground, representing the value their diligence can bring to a situation. Reliable almost to a fault, many Virgos will sacrifice their own needs to ensure others get what they need, but this can be a mistake for some, creating feelings of resentment if this isn't reciprocated. It can be a mistake too to expect that leading by

                                                       ♍   VIRGO

example will get the recognition it deserves, when instead Virgo's efforts get taken for granted. Inevitably there has to be a balance, and Virgos do need to ensure they don't overdo their efforts with a helping hand which can sometimes backfire, which isn't always welcomed.

Ruled by Mercury, Virgo is thoughtful and generally communicates with clarity, and can be quite precise and specific. Don't try and argue the facts with a Virgo, because they usually have these to hand: dates, times, places and what was said and who said what, are often easily recalled by the meticulous, detailed-oriented Virgo. Fortunately they are also grounded enough to realise that not everyone is as careful with information, and Virgo soon learns to accommodate and make allowances for what they see as others' sloppy relationship with this. The old adage, 'Do I want to be right, or happy?' was probably said by many a Virgo to themselves, having learnt that discretion is often the better part of valour.

Virgo is also gifted with a kind heart and seeks to make life better for their family, friends, work colleagues and lovers. Health in all its forms, spiritual, emotional and physical, is often a preoccupation for Virgo and they are the traditional caregivers, motivated by concern and practical sense. The only downside is that Virgo can sometimes feel relegated to the position of nurse or helper, the back-up and everyone's plan B, which doesn't always feel comfortable.

Again, it's important for Virgo to balance their instinct for caring for others with getting their own emotional and physical needs met. They can be the ultimate worriers of the zodiac – some Virgos are capable of turning it into an art form – and worrying about everything and everyone can take a toll on their own health. So Virgo needs to learn to manage these feelings and find a way to ground themselves in the reality of life. Being able to receive help from others can also be a learning curve for many Virgos, but their personal happiness very often depends on allowing others into their lives to love and support them in return.

THE MOON IN
YOUR CHART

While your zodiac sign is your sun sign, making you a sun sign Virgo, the Moon also plays a role in your birth chart and if you know the time and place of your birth, along with your birth date, you can get your birth chart done (see page 78). From this you can discover in which zodiac sign your Moon is positioned in your chart.

The Moon reflects the characteristics of who you are at the time of your birth, your innate personality, how you express yourself and how you are seen by others. This is in contrast to our sun sign, which indicates the more dominant characteristics we reveal as we travel through life. The Moon also represents the feminine in our natal chart (the Sun the masculine) and the sign in which our Moon falls can indicate how we express the feminine side of our personality. Looking at the two signs together in our charts immediately creates a balance.

MOON IN VIRGO

The Moon spends roughly 2.5 days in each zodiac sign as it moves through all 12 signs during its monthly cycle. This means that the Moon is regularly in Virgo, and it can be useful to know when this occurs and in particular when we have a New Moon or a Full Moon in Virgo because these are especially good times for you to focus your energy and intentions.

A New Moon is always the start of a new cycle, an opportunity to set new intentions for the coming month, and when this is in your own sign, Virgo, you can benefit from this additional energy and support. The Full Moon is an opportunity to reflect on the culmination of your earlier intentions.

NEW MOON
IN VIRGO AFFIRMATION

'Every day I will seek to be kind and extend
to myself the same kindness I extend to others, in
my thoughts, words and deeds.'

FULL MOON
IN VIRGO AFFIRMATION

'Every small step I make ensures my progress
and I believe in my ability to keep going
until I reach my journey's conclusion.'

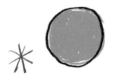

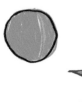

VIRGO HEALTH

Virgo rules the 6th House of health (see page 83) so it's not surprising that most take their own health seriously. Virgo rules abdominal health and the gut, and also the nervous system. The link between the gut and the nervous system is serotonin, some of which is produced by the brain but also by bacteria in the gut. Serotonin acts as a neurotransmitter and can help stabilise and improve mood, while an absence can predispose to anxiety and depression. Other problems that can affect Virgo include digestion problems, irritable bowel syndrome (IBS) and constipation.

Exercise is a feature of many Virgos' lives, not least because they recognise its considerable health benefits. They like to feel good physically and, in addition, many Virgos understand how this can help them manage fluctuations in mood. Plus, it's difficult to worry incessantly about the woes of the world while you're trying to prevent your opponent from scoring points or when you're pacing yourself at the gym. Even just walking briskly in the open air regularly, or a daily yoga practice, helps Virgo to shift focus away from their mind and into the body, breaking a cycle of repetitive thoughts and helping to restore energy levels and mood.

POWER UP
YOUR VIRGO
ENERGY

There are often moments or periods when we feel uninspired, demotivated and low in energy. At these times it's worth working with your innate sun sign energy to power up again, and paying attention to what Virgo relishes and needs can help support both physical and mental health.

Reconnecting with the earth is very restorative for Virgo and while one of the ways this can be done is through exercise, there are other activities like gardening, tending houseplants or a window box of herbs, which can help with that too. Even a hobby like open-air sketching or painting can be both rewarding and de-stressing for Virgo, helping to lighten and lift the mood by focusing on something that requires engagement and concentration and a shift in perspective.

Regular exercise is usually a way in which Virgo will seek to restore energy levels, and particularly if this has lapsed during a demanding period of work or illness, as they understand that when their body feels fit and strong again, their mind also benefits. In addition, in spite of all that nervous energy, as an earth sign Virgo is sometimes prone to sluggishness and weight gain, both of which can be helped by exercise. Of all the signs, Virgo understands better than most how the body and mind are connected, and many who may have struggled in the past to balance the two will have sought out and used yoga or meditative practices to help.

Many Virgos will also utilise their practical skills in the kitchen. The preparation of nutritious meals is restorative in itself but Virgos will find that a renewed focus on creating a delicious, balanced diet of fresh food, particularly during convalescence or after a period of junk food eating, really helps them. They may know this instinctively, but even the most fastidious Virgo sometimes needs reminding that eating regularly, without snacking in between, helps stabilise blood sugar levels and avoid feelings of nervous jitteriness and gut spasms. Making sure that carbohydrates are complex, with a low-glycaemic index, like oats, wholegrains, brown rice and vegetables, helps keep blood sugar levels stable, particularly if combined with good protein sources like lean chicken, fish, tofu and eggs, which also contain the amino acid tryptophan, from which serotonin is produced. Good dietary sources of vitamins and minerals are beneficial too, particularly magnesium which can be found in almonds, pumpkin seeds and spinach.

Utilise a New Moon in Virgo with a ritual to set your intentions and power up: light a candle, use essential oil of grapefruit to lift that earthy energy (this oil blends well with soothing chamomile and invigorating bergamot), focus your thoughts on the change you wish to see and allow time to meditate on this. Place your gemstone (see page 13) in the moonlight. Write down your intentions and keep in a safe place. Meditate on the New Moon in Virgo affirmation (see page 21).

At a Full Moon in Virgo you will have the benefit of the Sun's reflected light to help illuminate what is working for you and what you can let go, because the Full Moon brings clarity. Take the time to meditate on the Full Moon in Virgo affirmation (see page 21). Light a candle, place your gemstone in the moonlight and make a note of your thoughts and feelings, strengthened by the Moon in your sign.

VIRGO'S SPIRITUAL HOME

Knowing where to go to replenish your soul and recharge your batteries both physically and spiritually is important and worth serious consideration. For many Virgos, their garden, allotment or vegetable garden might be their spiritual home, where the earth's energy resonates with their own, or somewhere they've created, nurtured or cherished for themselves and others.

Wherever they hail from or end up, there are also a number of countries where Virgo will feel comfortable, whether they choose to go there to live, work or just take a holiday. These include the countries of Brazil, Ukraine, Switzerland and Mali, which all resonate with fertile Virgo energy.

When it comes to holidays, activity holidays often appeal: those connecting body to mind like beach yoga in Costa Rica, walking in the beauty of the Estonian countryside, or a cultural trip to the old city of Baku in Azerbaijan or the City of Angels, Los Angeles. All these places are linked to Virgo energy through Mercury's quickness of mind, grounded in the body.

VIRGO

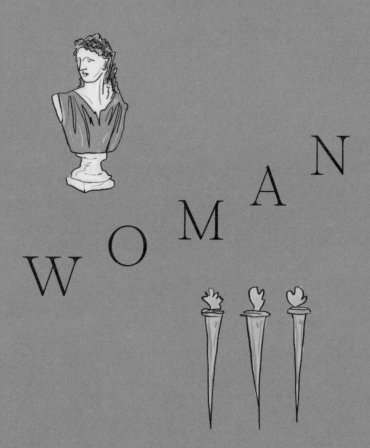

WOMAN

There's often something pleasingly precise about Virgo women in the way they dress and move. Whether they're in gym sweats or a designer suit, they always look well organised and polished. This may be a superficial thing and for many Virgo women it can hide a less organised internal life, but they know that good presentation is half the battle. For some, this can be the attraction of some sort of uniform, medical or military, that suggests discipline and conformity, something to which many Virgo women easily adapt. That's not to say that they don't have free-spirited, independent lives too, but there's often a predisposition to being organised because, as many of them will reason, it makes life easier if you're not constantly searching for lost house keys.

You can also rely on Virgo women to deliver on their promises. It's a matter of personal pride to many, but also because Virgo genuinely cares about other people and will go to some effort never to let anyone down, even occasionally to their own detriment. And this is something some Virgo women have a tendency to do, to be conscientious to a fault, with a streak of perfectionism. This can make life unnecessarily difficult, and if you constantly do everything today that anyone else would quite reasonably put off until tomorrow, it can be exhausting. Asking others for help is also something that doesn't come easily to many Virgo women, and they can end up feeling resentful when no one offers.

Generally of a happy and well-grounded disposition, Virgo women can sometimes come across as reserved, with a natural reticence, which can be misinterpreted as shyness or lack of confidence. This is seldom the case, but Virgo women often know the value of waiting to be sure of themselves so they don't inadvertently get things wrong. They can be very analytical and like to have time to get their facts straight, which avoids wasting time in the long run.

When it comes to a thoughtful response to a problem, Virgo women make the best friends. They are usually extremely good listeners and she will be more than happy to hear all the details, analyse them, and respond with good practical advice, whether this is about a love affair gone wrong, or a complicated work situation that needs a decision made. But Virgo women must also learn to allow others to return the favour, to help her when she needs it too, and accept gracefully.

V I R G O

N

A

M

There's something rather traditional about Virgo men. Their practical ability helps ensure they are recognised for their shelf-building skills as much as for their ability to change a tyre. Of course, there will be some Virgo men who are just as happy to organise someone else to do these things, but that's the clue: an ability to organise. And they will also get it done when it needs doing, rather than in a week or two, after they've been reminded several times. The truth is, they are never happier than when bringing order to chaos, solving problems and making life easier for those they care for. It's a lovely trait but can occasionally veer into the sort of conscientiousness where the newspaper has been recycled before everyone has read it.

Virgo man is also generally well organised in his appearance; he likes ironing his shirts (and even his underpants) and possibly has a colour-coded closet too. Or he has all his clothes the same colour so there's no time wasted in getting dressed. This is generally born from a desire to make life more efficient, so that he can get on with what really interests him. And he is likely to be a man with many interests, given that Mercury is his ruling planet, full of ideas and never bored. This isn't always obvious in someone who is often quite reticent in the way they approach life, and it may be quite hard to find out what Virgo man actually thinks, although you can be sure he has plenty of thoughts.

His kind heart means that he is seldom short of friends calling on him for assistance, and Virgo man is happy to be of service to those he loves, but also to hang out with him, as he is interesting company. As he matures, he will probably need to find a way to create the necessary boundaries to avoid being taken advantage of, utilising his Virgo adaptability to understand that it's sometimes better to help people learn to take care of themselves rather than to do everything for them. There's a grounded quality to his interactions that makes Virgo man a good teacher and he is able to communicate well thanks to his ruling planet Mercury.

VIRGO IN LOVE

It's not always obvious when a Virgo is in love, as they are generally not the type to go in for broadcasting their feelings. Instead, they prefer to be gently insistent until the object of their affections is in complete agreement. Virgo might be ruled by Mercury, but they aren't flighty in love; they are more grounded and sometimes so careful in their communications *d'amour* that it can be difficult for the recipient of their intentions to be sure whether or not this is a date or a work meeting, because Virgo may approach it initially in a similar way. However, once they have ticked their box, and they're sure they've limited the risk of rejection, then they can be as abundant in their declarations as anyone else. All of which might sound a bit boring, but for those who relish reliability in a lover, Virgo is a good choice.

VIRGO AS
A LOVER

For all their apparent reticence, Virgo is also a sign of great abundance and there's often a lovely sensuality and, thanks to being an earth sign, a good appreciation of the erotic. This might not be immediately apparent, not least because many Virgos consider spontaneity an overrated virtue, preferring instead to leave little to chance. But this has its own virtue, because being wooed by a Virgo is often so subtle and sensual that all their lover has to do is relax and enjoy, relying on them to take care of the rest.

Reliability is second nature to Virgo, which might sound rather dull and, much as they may like to be a more emotionally reckless type, this is their default. That's not to say that they will stick with someone if the relationship isn't going well; Virgo can be extremely straightforward in ending a love affair, going to some lengths to avoid messy endings. But their initial discrimination in choosing a partner means Virgo often makes good choices, as long as they avoid the trap of seeking to heal someone through love. That may happen but, as with all healthy relationships, it needs to be a two-way street.

Virgo often chooses a lover who is more sexually outgoing than they are, someone with whom they can express their more intimate feelings. There's an abundance of sexuality to be tapped in Virgos, just as soon as they overcome their reserve, which often happens as they mature and become more confident of the value of their sexual response. That tension between Virgo's body and mind is often overcome through sex, allowing them to relish the connection rather than keeping the two separate. Then they are the best of lovers, committed and engaged and loyal to their intimate partner.

  ♍

WHAT'S IN VIRGO'S BEDSIDE CABINET?

Beautifully laundered linen sheets, ready to be rumpled

A hand-stitched silk eye mask

An illustrated *Kama Sutra*

WHICH SIGN
SUITS VIRGO?

In relationships with Virgo, the sun sign of the other person and the ruling planet of that sign can bring out the best, or sometimes the worst, in a lover. Knowing what might spark, smoulder or suffocate love is worth closer investigation, but always remember that sun sign astrology is only a starting point for any relationship.

VIRGO
AND ARIES

Mercury and Mars have a similar physical energy that tends to attract sexually and as long as one doesn't try to overpower or outwit the other, this can be a harmonious match in which both can flourish and benefit.

VIRGO AND
TAURUS

Two earth signs that recognise the value of stability provide an immediate connection, while Mercury finds Venus very attractive and they tend to appreciate and bring out the best in each other, often making this a strong match.

VIRGO AND
GEMINI

Both ruled by Mercury, Virgo's earthy stability helps ground Gemini's flightier take on life and they both have the versatility to adapt, although there's a certain amount of compromise required on both sides to make secure a stable relationship.

40

♍ VIRGO

VIRGO AND CANCER

Cancer's more emotional Moon can sometimes irritate Virgo's pragmatic take on life, and this can lead to disagreements, but the water sign genuinely appreciates reliability as it makes them feel secure, and this can often seal the deal.

VIRGO AND LEO

Leo's enthusiastic nature attracts the more reticent Virgo, allowing them to warm and expand emotionally. Virgo enjoys the sunshine of Leo's attention, while in turn the fire sign enjoys a loving audience, often making this a very successful union.

VIRGO AND VIRGO

Together, these two may be too alike, competing for who worries most or who can take better care of the other, unless Mercury's intellectual side can provide the balance necessary to allow for the give and take necessary in a successful love match.

VIRGO
AND LIBRA

Libra loves a partnership and can easily find the balance necessary for a very successful relationship with caring Virgo, whose Mercury is attracted to Venus' charming and elegant ways, while their earthiness is lightened by Libra's air.

VIRGO AND
SCORPIO

Pluto's deep-thinking ways can sometimes overwhelm Virgo, particularly if it exacerbates their worries, although Scorpio can often transform the more negative side of this earth sign through the enduring commitment of their love.

VIRGO AND
SAGITTARIUS

Pragmatic Virgo often doesn't mind Sagittarius' need to come and go, both emotionally and physically, because Jupiter's general air of positivism does much to ease and allay Mercury's more worrying thoughts.

VIRGO AND CAPRICORN

Both these earth signs know the benefit of applying yourself in order to reap the rewards, although Mercury has a lighter touch, helping to balance Saturn's more stringent effect, allowing both signs to blossom in each other's company.

VIRGO AND AQUARIUS

Uranus may be unpredictable, but Virgo is versatile enough to accept this trait in Aquarius, and recognise that their commitment to the greater good of humanity reflects their own caring nature, and also includes a deep love for each other.

VIRGO AND PISCES

Virgo loves to take care of dreamy, imaginative Pisces, although there can be a temptation to overdo it and not ask for much in return, so honest communication helped by Mercury is important to ensure there's no feelings of resentment.

VIRGO AT
WORK

E veryone tends to love having a Virgo on their team. Not only do they get the job done, but it's usually done to the brief and on time. Seldom does a boss have to check whether or not Virgo is on task. They usually take real pride in excelling in their work, but Virgo may need to guard against the sort of perfectionism that can become a bad master rather than a good servant. A perfectionist attitude can also make delegating difficult and, for a career to progress, it's important not to get stuck at the do-it-all-yourself stage and learn to trust other people's work. Often, Virgo is such a good second-in-command, there's a resistance to promoting them into their own full leadership or executive role.

For such a welcome team player, Virgos are in fact some of the best at succeeding at a freelance or entrepreneurial career, purely because they are so good at organising their own time and delivering work to a consistently high standard. This is second nature to Virgo but what's also important, however, in whatever work Virgo chooses to do, is that they don't let this ability to be so precise and reliable stifle their creativity or prevent them taking risks to extend and develop their own careers.

Their attention to detail makes Virgo particularly good at careers that require this. Options like architecture or interior design, the law, book-keeping and accountancy can attract their brand of methodical creativity. Many Virgos also like to be hands-on, caring directly for others, so medicine or nursing which allows them to heal those in their care, is another career option many Virgos find attractive.

Wherever they choose to work, most Virgos like structure, even if it's self-imposed, and routine more than many other signs. Virgo just finds it easier to flourish within well-organised parameters, and they are likely to be great list-makers and box-tickers too. For most Virgos, money isn't a particular incentive, at least not initially, but they do like a good, reliable income and a nice lifestyle. They aren't by nature gamblers, but Virgos tend to do well financially, their diligence and canny investments being another benefit of Mercury's more meticulously researched influence.

VIRGO AT HOME

Home is significant to Virgo because it's where they can nourish others, whether family or housemates, and their hospitality is often very caring. There's always an unfussy welcome on the mat, with straightforward offers of a meal or bed for the night, should it be needed. When they say it's no problem, Virgo means it and they are disinclined to make a big fuss about it either. As housemates they are easy-going although they can take exception to extreme untidiness, or failure to take turns in cleaning the bath. If anyone draws up a list of weekly chores, it's likely to be Virgo.

Their home always seems to be in a state of readiness for an unexpected guest and this is reflected in Virgo's choice of furnishings, which tend to be comfortable. Virgos also tend to care about the health of planet Earth, so they are usually eco-conscious, with climate-protecting modifications made to their home. Warm and inviting, there can be a sensuality in the colours chosen, but what's also often noticeable is an absence of clutter: the tidy bookshelf, the folded laundry in the airing cupboard, the lack of washing-up in the sink. It's a relaxing home partly because it's also well organised and tidy, which is very much a Virgo trait, although it might infuriate housemates who can't find yesterday's newspaper to finish reading.

Ruling the 6th House of health is often evident in Virgo's home, which may include some gym equipment or even a sauna; they know how to improve their own health and wellbeing and often want to extend this to others. In fact, Virgo's bathroom may be given over to something of a spa, with a jacuzzi bath, soft lights and lots of healing oils and unguents to enjoy after a hard day's work. They like the practicality of a power shower as much as anyone, but Virgo also relishes the self-care that can compensate for the daily grind.

FREE THE
SPIRIT

Understanding your own sun sign astrology is only part of the picture. It provides you with a template to examine and reflect on your own life's journey but also the context for this through your relationships with others, intimate or otherwise, and within the culture and environment in which you live.

Throughout time, the Sun and planets of our universe have kept to their paths and astrologers have used this ancient wisdom to understand the pattern of the universe. In this way, astrology is a tool to utilise these wisdoms, a way of helping make sense of the energies we experience as the planets shift in our skies.

'A physician without a knowledge of astrology has no right to call himself a physician,' said Hippocrates, the Greek physician born in 460 BC, who understood better than anyone how these psychic energies worked. As did Carl Jung, the 20th-century philosopher and psychoanalyst, because he said, 'Astrology represents the summation of all the psychological knowledge of antiquity.'

SUN

Although the Sun is officially a star, for the purpose of astrology it's considered a planet. It is also the centre of our universe and gives us both light and energy; our lives are dependent on it and it embodies our creative life force. As a life giver, the Sun is considered a masculine entity, the patriarch and ruler of the skies. Our sun sign is where we start our astrological journey whichever sign it falls in, and as long as we know which day of which month we were born, we have this primary knowledge.

MOON

We now know that the Moon is actually a natural satellite of the Earth (the third planet from the Sun) rather than a planet but is considered such for the purposes of astrology. It's dependent on the Sun for its reflected light, and it is only through their celestial relationship that we can see it. In this way, the Moon in each of our birth charts depicts the feminine energy to balance the masculine Sun's life force, the ying to its yang. It is not an impotent or subservient presence, particularly when you consider how it gives the world's oceans their tides, the relentless energy of the ebb and flow powering up the seas. The Moon's energy also helps illuminate our unconscious desires, helping to bring these to the service of our self-knowledge.

MERCURY

RULES THE ASTROLOGICAL SIGNS OF GEMINI AND VIRGO

Mercury, messenger of the gods, has always been associated with speed and agility, whether in body or mind. Because of this, Mercury is considered to be the planet of quick wit and anything requiring verbal dexterity and the application of intelligence. Those with Mercury prominent in their chart love exchanging and debating ideas and telling stories (often with a tendency to embellish the truth of a situation), making them prominent in professions where these qualities are valuable.

Astronomically, Mercury is the closest planet to the Sun and moves around a lot in our skies. What's also relevant is that several times a year Mercury appears to be retrograde (see page 99) which has the effect of slowing down or disrupting its influence.

♍

VIRGO

VENUS

The goddess of beauty, love and pleasure. Venus is
the second planet from the Sun and benefits from
this proximity, having received its positive vibes.
Depending on which astrological sign Venus falls in
your chart will influence how you relate to art and
culture and the opposite sex. The characteristics of
this sign will tell you all you need to know about
what you aspire to, where you seek and how you
experience pleasure, along with the types of lover you
attract. Again, partly depending on where it's placed,
Venus can sometimes increase self-indulgence which
can be a less positive aspect of a hedonistic life.

MARS

This big, powerful planet is fourth from the Sun and exerts an energetic force, powering up the characteristics of the astrological sign in which it falls in your chart. This will tell you how you assert yourself, whether your anger flares or smoulders, what might stir your passion and how you express your sexual desires. Mars will show you what works best for you to turn ideas into action, the sort of energy you might need to see something through and how your independent spirit can be most effectively engaged.

JUPITER

Big, bountiful Jupiter is the largest planet in our solar
system and fifth from the Sun. It heralds optimism,
generosity and general benevolence. Whichever sign
Jupiter falls in in your chart is where you will find
the characteristics for your particular experience of
luck, happiness and good fortune. Jupiter will show
you which areas to focus on to gain the most and
best from your life. Wherever Jupiter appears in your
chart it will bring a positive influence and when it's
prominent in our skies we all benefit.

SATURN

Saturn is considered akin to Old Father Time, with all the patience, realism and wisdom that archetype evokes. Sometimes called the taskmaster of the skies, its influence is all about how we handle responsibility and it requires that we graft and apply ourselves in order to learn life's lessons. The sixth planet from the Sun, Saturn's 'return' (see page 100) to its place in an individual's birth chart occurs approximately every 28 years. How self-disciplined you are about overcoming opposition or adversity will be influenced by the characteristics of the sign in which this powerful planet falls in your chart.

URANUS

RULES THE ASTROLOGICAL SIGN OF AQUARIUS

The seventh planet from the Sun, Uranus is the
planet of unpredictability, change and surprise, and
whether you love or loathe the impact of Uranus
will depend in part on which astrological sign it
influences in your chart. How you respond to its
influence is entirely up to the characteristics of the
sign it occupies in your chart. Whether you see the
change it heralds as a gift or a curse is up to you, but
because it takes seven years to travel through a sign,
its presence in a sign can influence a generation.

  ♍ VIRGO

NEPTUNE

Neptune ruled the sea, and this planet is all about deep waters of mystery, imagination and secrets. It's also representative of our spiritual side so the characteristics of whichever astrological sign it occupies in your chart will influence how this plays out in your life. Neptune is the eighth planet from the Sun and its influence can be subtle and mysterious. The astrological sign in which it falls in your chart will indicate how you realise your vision, dream and goals. The only precaution is if it falls in an equally watery sign, creating a potential difficulty in distinguishing between fantasy and reality.

PLUTO

Pluto is the furthest planet from the Sun and exerts
a regenerative energy that transforms but often
requires destruction to erase what's come before in
order to begin again. Its energy often lies dormant
and then erupts, so the astrological sign in which it
falls will have a bearing on how this might play out in
your chart. Transformation can be very positive but
also very painful. When Pluto's influence is strong,
change occurs and how you react or respond to this
will be very individual. Don't fear it, but reflect on
how to use its energy to your benefit.

YOUR SUN SIGN

Your sun or zodiac sign is the one in which you were born, determined by the date of your birth. Your sun sign is ruled by a specific planet. For example, Virgo is ruled by Mercury but Aquarius by Uranus, so we already have the first piece of information and the first piece of our individual jigsaw puzzle.

The next piece of the jigsaw is understanding that the energy of a particular planet in your birth chart (see page 78) plays out via the characteristics of the astrological sign in which it's positioned, and this is hugely valuable in understanding some of the patterns of your life. You may have your Sun in Virgo, and a good insight into the characteristics of this sign, but what if you have Neptune in Leo? Or Venus in Aries? Uranus in Virgo? Understanding the impact of these influences can help you reflect on the way you react or respond and the choices you can make, helping to ensure more positive outcomes.

If, for example, with Uranus in Taurus you are resistant to change, remind yourself that change is inevitable and can be positive, allowing you to work with it rather than against its influence. If you have Neptune in Virgo, it will bring a more spiritual element to this practical earth sign, while Mercury in Aquarius will enhance the predictive element of your analysis and judgement. The scope and range and useful aspect of having this knowledge is just the beginning of how you can utilise astrology to live your best life.

PLANETS IN TRANSIT

In addition, the planets do not stay still. They are said to transit (move) through the course of an astrological year. Those closest to us, like Mercury, transit quite regularly (every 88 days), while those further away, like Pluto, take much longer, in this case 248 years to come full circle. So the effects of each planet can vary depending on their position and this is why we hear astrologers talk about someone's Saturn return (see page 100), Mercury retrograde (see page 99) or about Capricorn (or other sun sign) 'weather'. This is indicative of an influence that can be anticipated and worked with and is both universal and personal. The shifting positions of the planets bring an influence to bear on each of us, linked to the position of our own planetary influences and how these have a bearing on each other. If you understand the nature of these planetary influences you can begin to work with, rather than against, them and this information can be very much to your benefit. First, though, you need to take a look at the component parts of astrology, the pieces of your personal jigsaw, then you'll have the information you need to make sense of how your sun sign might be affected during the changing patterns of the planets.

YOUR BIRTH CHART

With the date, time and place of birth, you can easily find out where your (or anyone else's) planets are positioned from an online astrological chart programme (see page 110). This will give you an exact sun sign position, which you probably already know, but it can also be useful if you think you were born 'on the cusp' because it will give you an *exact* indication of what sign you were born in. In addition, this natal chart will tell you your Ascendant sign, which sign your Moon is in, along with the other planets specific to your personal and completely individual chart and the Houses (see page 81) in which the astrological signs are positioned.

A birth chart is divided into 12 sections, representing each of the 12 Houses (see pages 82–85) with your Ascendant or Rising sign always positioned in the 1st House, and the other 11 Houses running counter-clockwise from one to 12.

ASCENDANT OR RISING SIGN

Your Ascendant is a first, important part of the complexity of an individual birth chart. While your sun sign gives you an indication of the personality you will inhabit through the course of your life, it is your Ascendant or Rising sign – which is the sign rising at the break of dawn on the Eastern horizon at the time and on the date of your birth – that often gives a truer indication of how you will project your personality and consequently how the world sees you. So even though you were born a sun sign Virgo, whatever sign your Ascendant is in, for example Cancer, will be read through the characteristics of this astrological sign.

Your Ascendant is always in your 1st House, which is the House of the Self (see page 82) and the other houses always follow the same consecutive astrological order. So if, for example, your Ascendant is Leo, then your second house is in Virgo, your third house in Libra, and so on. Each house has its own characteristics but how these will play out in your individual chart will be influenced by the sign positioned in it.

Opposite your Ascendant is your Descendant sign, positioned in the 7th House (see page 84) and this shows what you look for in a partnership, your complementary 'other half' as it were. There's always something intriguing about what the Descendant can help us to understand, and it's worth knowing yours and being on the lookout for it when considering a long-term marital or business partnership.

THE
12
HOUSES

While each of the 12 Houses represent different aspects of our lives, they are also ruled by one of the 12 astrological signs, giving each house its specific characteristics. When we discover, for example, that we have Capricorn in the 12th House, this might suggest a pragmatic or practical approach to spirituality. Or, if you had Gemini in your 6th House, this might suggest a rather airy approach to organisation.

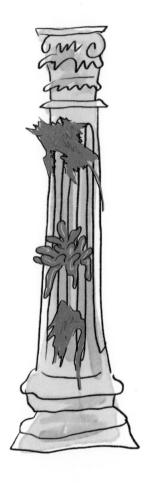

1ST HOUSE

RULED BY ARIES

The first impression you give walking into
a room, how you like to be seen, your sense
of self and the energy with which you
approach life.

2ND HOUSE

RULED BY TAURUS

What you value, including what you own
that provides your material security; your
self-value and work ethic, how you earn
your income.

3RD HOUSE

RULED BY GEMINI

How you communicate through words,
deeds and gestures; also how you learn and
function in a group, including within your
own family.

4TH HOUSE

RULED BY CANCER

This is about your home, your security
and how you take care of yourself and
your family; and also about those family
traditions you hold dear.

5TH HOUSE

RULED BY LEO

Creativity in all its forms, including fun
and eroticism, intimate relationships and
procreation, self-expression
and positive fulfilment.

6TH HOUSE

RULED BY VIRGO

How you organise your daily routine, your
health, your business affairs, and how you
are of service to others, from those
in your family to the workplace.

7 TH HOUSE

RULED BY LIBRA

This is about partnerships and shared
goals, whether marital or in business,
and what we look for in these to
complement ourselves.

8 TH HOUSE

RULED BY SCORPIO

Regeneration, through death and rebirth,
and also our legacy and how this might be
realised through sex, procreation
and progeny.

9 TH HOUSE

RULED BY SAGITTARIUS

Our world view, cultures outside our
own and the bigger picture beyond our
immediate horizon, to which we travel
either in body or mind.

10TH HOUSE

RULED BY CAPRICORN

Our aims and ambitions in life, what we
aspire to and what we're prepared to do
to achieve it; this is how we approach our
working lives.

11TH HOUSE

RULED BY AQUARIUS

The house of humanity and our
friendships, our relationships with the
wider world, our tribe or group to which
we feel an affiliation.

12TH HOUSE

RULED BY PISCES

Our spiritual side resides here. Whether this
is religious or not, it embodies our inner
life, beliefs and the deeper connections
we forge.

THE FOUR ELEMENTS

The 12 astrological signs are divided into four groups, representing the four elements: fire, water, earth and air. This gives each of the three signs in each group additional characteristics.

FIRE

ARIES ❧ LEO ❧ SAGITTARIUS

Embodying warmth, spontaneity and enthusiasm.

♍

VIRGO

WATER

CANCER ❧ SCORPIO ❧ PISCES

Embodying a more feeling, spiritual and intuitive side.

EARTH

TAURUS ~ VIRGO ~ CAPRICORN

Grounded and sure-footed and sometimes rather stubborn.

AIR

GEMINI ⚭ LIBRA ⚭ AQUARIUS

Flourishing in the world of vision, ideas and perception.

FIXED, CARDINAL OR MUTABLE?

The 12 signs are further divided into three groups of four, giving additional characteristics of being fixed, cardinal or mutable. These represent the way in which they respond to situations.

FIXED

TAURUS, LEO, SCORPIO AND AQUARIUS ARE FIXED SIGNS

Their energy tends to be steady and they are less reactive, more responsive, although they can have a tendency to be resistant to change and need encouragement.

CARDINAL

ARIES, CANCER, LIBRA AND CAPRICORN ARE CARDINAL SIGNS

Their energy is often instinctive and action-oriented, enabling them to get things started, although there's sometimes a tendency to fail to carry things through.

MUTABLE

GEMINI, VIRGO, SAGITTARIUS AND PISCES ARE MUTABLE SIGNS

The clue here is their adaptability and responsiveness to change, which they don't fear, and readiness to listen to and embrace new ideas.

MERCURY RETROGRADE

This occurs several times over the astrological year and lasts for around four weeks, with a shadow week either side (a quick Google search will tell you the forthcoming dates). It's important what sign Mercury is in while it's retrograde, because its impact will be affected by the characteristics of that sign. For example, if Mercury is retrograde in Gemini, the sign of communication that is ruled by Mercury, the effect will be keenly felt in all areas of communication. However, if Mercury is retrograde in Aquarius, which rules the house of friendships and relationships, this may keenly affect our communication with large groups, or if in Sagittarius, which rules the house of travel, it could affect travel itineraries and encourage us to check our documents carefully.

Mercury retrograde can also be seen as an opportunity to pause, review or reconsider ideas and plans, to regroup, recalibrate and recuperate, and generally to take stock of where we are and how we might proceed. In our fast-paced 24/7 lives, Mercury retrograde can often be a useful opportunity to slow down and allow ourselves space to restore some necessary equilibrium.

SATURN RETURN

When the planet Saturn returns to the place in your chart that it occupied at the time of your birth, it has an impact. This occurs roughly every 28 years, so we can see immediately that it correlates with ages that we consider representative of different life stages and when we might anticipate change or adjustment to a different era. At 28 we can be considered at full adult maturity, probably established in our careers and relationships, maybe with children; at 56 we have reached middle age and are possibly at another of life's crossroads; and at 84, we might be considered at the full height of our wisdom, our lives almost complete. If you know the time and place of your birth date, an online Saturn return calculator can give you the exact timing.

It will also be useful to identify in which astrological sign Saturn falls in your chart, which will help you reflect on its influence, as both influences can be very illuminating about how you will experience and manage the impact of its return. Often the time leading up to a personal Saturn return is a demanding one, but the lessons learnt help inform the decisions made about how to progress your own goals. Don't fear this period, but work with its influence: knowledge is power and Saturn has a powerful energy you can harness should you choose.

♍

THE MINOR PLANETS

Sun sign astrology seldom makes mention of these 'minor' planets that also orbit the sun, but increasingly their subtle influence is being referenced. If you have had your birth chart done (if you know your birth time and place you can do this online) you will have access to this additional information.

Like the 10 main planets on the previous pages, these 18 minor entities will also be positioned in an astrological sign, bringing their energy to bear on these characteristics. You may, for example, have Fortuna in Leo, or Diana in Sagittarius. Look to these for their subtle influences on your birth chart and life via the sign they inhabit, all of which will serve to animate and resonate further the information you can reference on your own personal journey.

AESCULAPIA

Jupiter's grandson and a powerful healer, Aesculapia was taught by Chiron and influences us in what could be life-saving action, realised through the characteristics of the sign in which it falls in our chart.

BACCHUS

Jupiter's son, Bacchus is similarly benevolent but can sometimes lack restraint in the pursuit of pleasure. How this plays out in your chart is dependent on the sign in which it falls.

APOLLO

Jupiter's son, gifted in art, music and healing, Apollo rides the Sun across the skies. His energy literally lights up the way in which you inspire others, characterised by the sign in which it falls in your chart.

CERES

Goddess of agriculture and mother of Proserpina, Ceres is associated with the seasons and how we manage cycles of change in our lives. This energy is influenced by the sign in which it falls in our chart.

CHIRON

Teacher of the gods, Chiron knew all about healing herbs and medical practices and he lends his energy to how we tackle the impossible or the unthinkable, that which seems difficult to do.

DIANA

Jupiter's independent daughter was allowed to run free without the shackles of marriage. Where this falls in your birth chart will indicate what you are not prepared to sacrifice in order to conform.

CUPID

Son of Venus. The sign into which Cupid falls will influence how you inspire love and desire in others, not always appropriately and sometimes illogically but it can still be an enduring passion.

FORTUNA

Jupiter's daughter, who is always shown blindfolded, influences your fated role in other people's lives, how you show up for them without really understanding why, and at the right time.

♍

HYGEIA

Daughter of Aesculapia and also associated with health, Hygeia is about how you anticipate risk and the avoidance of unwanted outcomes. The way you do this is characterised by the sign in which Hygeia falls.

MINERVA

Another of Jupiter's daughters, depicted by an owl, will show you via the energy given to a particular astrological sign in your chart how you show up at your most intelligent and smart. How you operate intellectually.

JUNO

Juno was the wife of Jupiter and her position in your chart will indicate where you will make a commitment in order to feel safe and secure. It's where you might seek protection in order to flourish.

OPS

The wife of Saturn, Ops saved the life of her son Jupiter by giving her husband a stone to eat instead of him. Her energy in our chart enables us to find positive solutions to life's demands and dilemmas.

PANACEA

Gifted with healing powers, Panacea
provides us with a remedy for all ills
and difficulties, and how this plays
out in your life will depend on the
characteristics of the astrological sign
in which her energy falls.

PSYCHE

Psyche, Venus' daughter-in-law, shows
us that part of ourselves that is easy to
love and endures through adversity,
and your soul that survives death and
flies free, like the butterfly that
depicts her.

PROSERPINA

Daughter of Ceres, abducted by Pluto,
Proserpina has to spend her life divided
between earth and the underworld and
she represents how we bridge the gulf
between different and difficult aspects
of our lives.

SALACIA

Neptune's wife, Salacia stands on
the seashore bridging land and sea,
happily bridging the two realities.
In your chart, she shows how you
can harmoniously bring two sides of
yourself together.

VESTA

Daughter of Saturn, Vesta's job was to protect Rome and in turn she was protected by vestal virgins. Her energy influences how we manage our relationships with competitive females and male authority figures.

VULCAN

Vulcan was a blacksmith who knew how to control fire and fashion metal into shape, and through the sign in which it falls in your chart will show you how you control your passion and make it work for you.

FURTHER READING

Jung's Studies in Astrology: Prophecies, Magic and the Qualities of Time,

Liz Greene, Routledge (2018)

Lunar Oracle: Harness the Power of the Moon,

Liberty Phi, OH Editions (2021)

Metaphysics of Astrology: Why Astrology Works,

Ivan Antic, Independently published (2020)

Parkers' Astrology: The Definitive Guide to Using Astrology in Every Aspect of Your Life,

Julia and Derek Parker, Dorling Kindersley (2020)

USEFUL WEBSITES

Alicebellastrology.com
Astro.com
Astrology.com
Cafeastrology.com
Costarastrology.com
Jessicaadams.com

USEFUL APPS

Astro Future
Co-Star
Moon
Sanctuary
Time Nomad
Time Passages

ACKNOWLEDGEMENTS

Thanks are due to my Taurean publisher Kate Pollard for commissioning this Astrology Oracle series, to Piscean Matt Tomlinson for his careful editing, and to Evi O Studio for their beautiful design and illustrations.

ABOUT THE AUTHOR

As a sun sign Aquarius Liberty Phi loves to explore the world and has lived on three different continents, currently residing in North America. Their Gemini moon inspires them to communicate their love of astrology and other esoteric practices while Leo rising helps energise them. Their first publication, also released by OH Editions, is a box set of 36 oracle cards and accompanying guide, entitled *Lunar Oracle: Harness the Power of the Moon*.

Published in 2023 by OH Editions,
an imprint of Welbeck Non-Fiction Ltd,
part of the Welbeck Publishing Group.
Offices in London, 20 Mortimer Street, London, W1T 3JW,
and Sydney, 205 Commonwealth Street, Surry Hills, 2010.
www.welbeckpublishing.com

Design © 2023 OH Editions
Text © 2023 Liberty Phi
Illustrations © 2023 Evi O. Studio

A CIP catalogue record for this book is available from the British Library.

ISBN 978-1-91431-798-9

Publisher: Kate Pollard
Editor: Sophie Elletson
In-house editor: Matt Tomlinson
Designer: Evi O. Studio
Illustrator: Evi O. Studio
Production controller: Jess Brisley
Printed and bound by Leo Paper

10 9 8 7 6 5 4 3 2 1